52
SUGAR
FREE
◆ DESSERTS ◆

JOAN MARY ALIMONTI

First Edition

QUICKLINE PUBLICATIONS
P.O. Box 23362
Pleasant Hill, CA 94523-0362

First Printing: March 1989
Typing: Becky Styles
Editing: Elizabeth A. Romano
Cover & Book Design: Dominic DiMento

Quickline Publications
P.O. Box 23362
Pleasant Hill, CA 94523-0362

J oan Mary Alimonti

lost 60 pounds in 1970 and has maintained her weight loss ever since.

When she achieved her goal, she realized she had to change her ways. She cut down on fat and added lots of vegetables to her daily meals. "Creative cooking and eating" became her focus. Joan describes herself as a cook — not a gourmet cook, but a California ad libber — a creative cook, if you will. "I understand food and I like to create what I call flexible recipes."

As a result of her culinary efforts, she published her first recipe collection in 1979. The "I Love to Eat but Hate to Diet Cookbook" has sold over 30,000 copies to date.

Joan is active in Northern California, giving food demonstrations and as a weight control meeting leader for a worldwide weight loss organization. The idea for "52 Sugar Free Desserts" developed out of her quest to create nutritious, delicious low-calorie foods and a recognition of the unique needs of diabetics.

She and her husband are presently putting the finishing touches on a new wood and glass home which Joan designed in Pioneer, California.

Joan believes a good balance of exercise for the body and challenge for the mind are important elements of good health. A positive attitude makes for happy people who achieve their goals.

I dedicate this cookbook to some of the most successful people I know:

Robin Agostino Mary Aldrich Barbara Armstrong Emily Bach Dori Bailey
Janet Baker Maureen Barry Al Bartz Arlene Beckman Audrey Mariana
Behdjet Carrie Besso Lois Bestor Ellana Blau Mary Jo Bonnell Christine
Botti Linda Bowling Ardath Brandley Carol Breenley Julie Bretz Carolyn
Brittian Susan Brudney John Burns Linda Byers Judy Calcagno Jim
Campbell Mary Cerri Virginia Christopher Maureen Cling Janie Cockman
Tracy Colbert Jeanne Colson Robert Coney Marlene Cook Claudia Correia
Jeanette Cox Pat Cunningham Verna Custer Janice Dalton Pamela Daulton
Donna Davis Carolyn Daw Chris DeFabio Diane Delucchi Jan Dickerson
Ellen Dietschy Lisa Donaldson Mindy Dopler-Nelson Jenny Dragonetti
Patty Duffy Ilene Dulkin Becky Dunn John Edwards Beth Eichenberger Pat
Escalambre Chris De Fabio Ellen Fasso Diane Fenchel Claudine Fletcher
Loie Fletcher Doris Foskett Joan Fowle Wilma Franzone Charlene Fuller
Steve Furtado B. J. Gerth Rachel Glaeser Anita Glass Esther Goff Rosemary
Grasso Roddy Greenblatt Sharon Groh Gary Grover Sandy Gsand Karen
Hansen Kathy Hanson Marsha Harris Dianne Haworth Norma Helles Pat
Herrera Beth Higdon Marian Hollar Bobbie Homan Mary Frances Horan
Peggie Howell Sharon Hunsinger Helene Hunter Janet James Linda Jimenez
Elvina Jones Harriett Kantor Kristine Kastl Karen Keegan Jini Kelley Debbie
Kennedy Norma Kilpatrick Nancy Klim Susan Knop Janie Krohn Carol
Kumer JoAnn Lancaster Marilyn Larson Linda Lasher Lorraine Leatham
Donna Lee Bonne Lenz Lisa Levitt Sheila Lewis Sheila Lewis Ro Liebson
Gina Long Kathy Lott Rosario Luttrell Sandi Maack Liz Mann Patricia
McCallister Virginia McCormick Juanita McCoy Marianne McCraney
Nancy McEachern Jeanne McGowan Joan Meloy Robert Michalske Marcia
Miller Cathy Milner Tracey Norton Moore Marge Mora Tony Mora Paula
Mora Pat Mosher Wanda O'Dell Linda Ogeden Nancy Ortiz Becky
Overstreet Karen Paranteau Lois Perdue Donna Peterson Linda Piscitelli
Ann Pistole Carlotta Priesto Michael Proctor Pat Rae Marjorie Rebrovich
Agnes Riccobuono Joann Riener Paula Robb Libby Rodighiero Kay Romero
Alice Ropchan Kathleen Rose Patti Ross Marybeth Saari Donna Schor
Nancy Schreiber Joyce Sellers Esther Seppanen Mary Shepherd Janice Shield
Nancy Siegel Arlene Silvas Judy Simpson Felicitas Sinosky Florence
Sokoloff John Soza Ina Speer Sue Standridge Caron Stitzinger Pat Straub
Nancy Swart Sylvia Taylor Nancy Teese Stephanie Thomas Zelda Thomas
Florence Thompson Cathie Treulich Helen Turley Cathy Turnbaugh
Margaret Turner Wilma Van Aken Connie Van Scyoc Brigitte Walker Jane
Weinheimer Kay Westerlund George Westerlund Bobbie Wexenberg Carol
Weyer Mariana Wheeler Audrey Whiteman Perla Wicaner Becky Willis
Linda Windisch Jennifer Winsborrow Kay Wisdom Connie Wojcik Leslie
Yakaitis Lela Young Mimi Zinn

—J.M.A.

Food is to be enjoyed! Proper nutrition doesn't just happen — we create it; we learn it; we live it. Now, with this cookbook, desserts and baked goods can be part of your lifestyle without guilt.

This book provides an opportunity for the diabetic and those looking for weight loss and/or weight control to take a front seat in this world of good eating.

NO SUGARS, NO WHITE FLOUR, LOW FAT AND PROPER FOOD PORTIONS. Enjoy! Be happy — a healthy person is a happy person.

A Word About Nutrition In General

Nutrition is defined as the process by which we utilize foods in order to maintain healthy bodily functions. Foods provide the nutrients necessary for energy, growth, and repair of body tissues, as well as for regulation and control of body processes. You need about 40 different nutrients to stay healthy; these include proteins, fats, carbohydrates, vitamins, minerals and water. It is the amount of proteins, carbohydrates, and fats in foods that determines their energy value (caloric content). Everyone needs the same nutrients each day in varying amounts based on age, sex, size, activity and state of health. Nutritionists agree that good health is promoted by keeping track of total caloric intake each day and dividing it into 20% proteins, 50% carbohydrates (most of which should be complex — 3/4 grains and starches compared with 1/4 fruits and vegetables), and 30% fat.

Variety is the key to success. No single food supplies all the essential nutrients in the amounts needed. The greater the variety of food, the less likely you are to develop either a deficiency or an excess of any single nutrient, and the more interesting and attractive your diet will be.

Specifically For Diabetics

Proper nutrition is the foundation of optimum health and essential for everyone, especially diabetics. All nutrients, including the desserts in this book, must fit into your physician's or dietician's program tailored especially to meet your needs. CHECK WITH YOUR PHYSICIAN OR DIETICIAN TO VERIFY THE APPROPRIATENESS OF THESE RECIPES IN YOUR FOOD PLAN.

Exchange Information

There are six categories of food: proteins, breads, fruits, milk, fats and vegetables. Except for vegetables, which are generally unlimited, all the others are to be used in specific portions each day. An exchange is a specific measure or amount of food which can be exchanged for a similar food within the same category. We need a certain number of exchanges each day to meet our nutrient needs.

Protein	6 exchanges (female)
	8 exchanges (male/child)
Bread	3 exchanges (female)
	5 exchanges (male/child)
Fruit	3 exchanges (female)
	5 exchanges (male/child)
Milk	2 exchanges (male/female)
	4 exchanges (child)
Fat	3 exchanges (all)

For variety and recipe development 70 optional calories are also available each day. Those not used can be saved for another day.

Although there are complete lists of exchanges in the American Diatetic System, here is a list of the exchanges used in this book. There are many mix-and-match opportunities.

1 protein exchange =	1 egg
	1/4 cup part-skim ricotta
	1/3 cup low-fat cottage cheese
	1 oz. hard cheese
1 bread exchange =	1 slice bread (80 calories)
	3 tablespoons flour
	2 graham crackers (2 1/2 squares)
	1/2 cup cooked rice
	1/2 cup cooked pasta
	3/4 ounce dry cereal or before cooking
1 fat exchange =	1 teaspoon vegetable oil margarine
	2 teaspoons reduced calorie vegetable oil margarine
	1 teaspoon vegetable oil
	1 teaspoon mayonnaise
	2 teaspoons reduced calorie mayonnaise

1 fruit exchange =	1 small apple
	1/3 cup apple juice
	1/2 cup applesauce
	4 dried apricots (halves)
	2 medium apricots
	1 small banana
	1/2 cup blueberries
	1 cup fresh cranberries
	2 dates
	1 medium kiwi
	1 small nectarine
	1 small orange
	1/2 cup orange juice
	2 tablespoons frozen orange juice concentrate
	1 small peach
	2 medium plums
	2 large prunes
	2 tablespoons raisins
	1/2 cup raspberries
	1 cup strawberries

(All canned/frozen to be unsweetened)

1 milk exchange =	1 cup fluid skim/nonfat
	1/3 cup nonfat <u>dry</u> powdered
	1/2 cup skim evaporated
	1/2 cup low-fat plain yogurt
	3/4 cup buttermilk
	2 tablespoons dry buttermilk powder
	1 packet sugar-free flavored milk beverage

Extra calories	10 calories =	2 teaspoons cocoa, un-sweetened powdered
		1 teaspoon cornstarch
		1/2 egg white
	50 calories =	1 tablespoon whipping cream

Sugar-free diet foods - see label.

If you have special dietary restrictions due to high cholesterol, you may use 1/4 cup egg substitute for each egg; or, in some recipes, using just the egg white works well.

Reduced calorie vegetable oil margarine saves fat calories. There is twice as much fat in regular vegetable oil.

I always write dessert recipes keeping fats and breads to a minimum, since these exchanges are needed for daily meals.

Plumping raisins before using insures a more moist product.

Low-calorie flavored milk beverage may be found in the dried milk section of your supermarket.

Dry buttermilk powder adds volume to dry ingredients. It can be found in the baking ingredients section of the supermarket or in bulk form in natural food stores. Liquid buttermilk is usually in the dairy section.

I like to use canned pumpkin. It is lower in calories than most vegetables and is a good source of dietary fiber, making it a great ingredient.

Mixing with a whisk is the easiest way to blend in dry ingredients.

Pastry made from whole wheat flour is very different in taste and texture. Give it a try in the pie and tart recipes and keep an open mind. You may, if you like, use white flour. The same recipes will yield the pastry with which you are familiar.

Using a metal cake pan with a 360° rotating metal slide on the bottom removes the cake with ease.

— J. M. A.

CONTENTS

♦ CAKES & TORTES ♦

♦ COOKIES, BARS & BROWNIES ♦

♦ DESSERT BREADS & COFFEE CAKES ♦

◆ PIES & TARTS ◆

◆ PUDDINGS & COBBLERS ◆

◆ MUFFINS ◆

◆ INTERNATIONAL FAVORITES ◆

◆ EXTRA SPECIAL EXTRA ◆

·1·

Cakes
&
Tortes

◆ GREAT CHOCOLATE CAKE ◆
With Banana Cream Filling and Whipped Topping

1 1/2 cups whole wheat flour
1/4 cup unsweetened cocoa powder
3/4 cup SugarTwin®* brown sugar substitute
1 tablespoon baking powder
2 teaspoons baking soda
1/4 teaspoon salt
2 eggs, beaten
1/3 cup reduced calorie vegetable oil margarine
   at room temperature
1/3 cup reduced calorie mayonnaise
1 1/2 cups buttermilk
1 teaspoon vanilla

BANANA CREAM FILLING

1 cup plain low-fat yogurt
2 packets Equal®** sweetener
1/2 teaspoon vanilla
1 large banana
1/2 pint whipped cream
1 small package sugar-free instant banana pudding

EXCHANGES

Each serving:
   1/4 protein exchange
   1 bread exchange
   1/2 fruit exchange
   3/4 milk exchange
   2 fat exchanges
   58 extra calories (50 belong to whipped cream)

---

* SugarTwin® is the registered trademark of The Alberto-Culver Company.
** Equal® is the registered trademark of NutraSweet for its brand of sweetening ingredient.

You think you can't make a great chocolate cake with whole wheat flour? Well, think again and be ready for a wonderful surprise.

In a large bowl:
- 1 1/2 cups whole wheat flour
- 1/4 cup unsweetened cocoa powder
- 3/4 cup SugarTwin® brown sugar substitute
- 1 tablespoon baking powder
- 2 teaspoons baking soda
- 1/4 teaspoon salt

Stir with a whisk to combine.

In another large bowl:
- 2 eggs, beaten
- 1/3 cup reduced calorie vegetable oil margarine at room temperature
- 1/3 cup reduced calorie mayonnaise
- 1 1/2 cups buttermilk
- 1 teaspoon vanilla

Combine thoroughly. Add flour mixture and beat with electric mixer. Pour into two 8-inch cake pans sprayed with nonstick cooking spray. Bake at 350° for 20–25 minutes or until a wooden pick comes out clean. Cool in pan 5–10 minutes; remove cake from pan and set on wire rack to cool.

BANANA CREAM FILLING
Following directions, make up 1 small package sugar-free instant banana pudding. Remove 1/2 of mixture for some other use.

To the remaining 1/2 mixture add:
- 1 cup plain low-fat yogurt
- 2 packets Equal® sweetener
- 1/2 teaspoon vanilla

Mix well and refrigerate.

To assemble cake:

Place one cake on plate. Spread banana pudding mixture on top. Slice a large banana into thin rounds and press them into the banana mixture. Place remaining cake on top. Decorate top with whipped cream (1/2 pint whipped with Equal® sweetener) and a large sliced banana.

◆ AUNT MILLIE'S BANANA CAKE ◆

4 large very ripe bananas
2 eggs, beaten
2 tablespoons plus 2 teaspoons vegetable oil
1 teaspoon vanilla
1 1/2 cups whole wheat flour
2/3 cup nonfat dry powdered milk
1/2 cup SugarTwin® brown sugar substitute
1 teaspoon baking soda
1 teaspoon baking powder
1/2 teaspoon cinnamon
whipped cream (optional)

EXCHANGES

Each serving:
1/4 protein exchange
1 bread exchange
1 fruit exchange
1/4 milk exchange
1 fat exchange

Oops!! Bananas too ripe? What a great excuse to make this best ever banana experience.

In a large bowl:
  4 large very ripe bananas
Beat with electric mixer until smooth.

Add:
  2 eggs, beaten
  2 tablespoons plus 2 teaspoons vegetable oil
  1 teaspoon vanilla
Beat well to combine.

Add:
  1 1/2 cups whole wheat flour
  2/3 cup nonfat dry powdered milk
  1/2 cup SugarTwin® brown sugar substitute
  1 teaspoon baking soda
  1 teaspoon baking powder
  1/2 teaspoon cinnamon
Beat with mixer to combine thoroughly.

Pour into 8-inch round or 8 x 8-inch baking dish sprayed with nonstick cooking spray. Bake at 350° for 20–25 minutes or until wooden pick comes out clean.

Cool for 10 minutes, then turn out on rack to cool completely. Foil wrap and refrigerate until ready to use.

Serve with whipped cream (optional).

◆ ORANGE SUNSHINE CAKE ◆
With Creamy Cheese Filling and Topping

1 1/2 cups whole wheat flour
3 teaspoons baking powder
4 eggs
3/4 cup SugarTwin® brown sugar substitute
1/3 cup reduced calorie vegetable oil margarine
1/2 cup frozen orange juice concentrate
1/4 cup sugar-free orange marmalade
1 cup plain low-fat yogurt
1 1/2 teaspoons vanilla

CREAMY CHEESE FILLING

1 cup part-skim ricotta cheese
6 tablespoons orange juice concentrate
8 packets Equal® sweetener
1/2 cup orange sections

EXCHANGES

Each serving cake with filling:
1 protein exchange
1 bread exchange
1 fruit exchange
1/4 milk exchange
1 fat exchange
6 extra calories

Make any day full of sunshine with this cake. What a great way to get your Vitamin C.

In a medium bowl:
  1 1/2 cups whole wheat
    flour
  3 teaspoons baking powder
Stir with whisk to combine.

In a large bowl:
  4 eggs
  3/4 cup SugarTwin® brown
    sugar substitute
Beat at high speed for 10
  minutes.

In a small bowl:
  1/3 cup reduced calorie
    vegetable oil margarine,
    melted and cooled
  1/2 cup frozen orange juice
    concentrate
  1/4 cup sugar-free orange
    marmalade
  1 cup plain low-fat yogurt
  1 1/2 teaspoons vanilla
Stir to combine.

Gently fold flour mixture into egg mixture; then fold in yogurt mixture. Mix until well blended.

Pour into two 8-inch cake pans sprayed with nonstick cooking spray. Bake at 350° for 20–25 minutes until wooden pick comes out clean. Cool in pan on rack for 5 minutes. Remove from pan and finish cooling on racks.

CREAMY CHEESE FILLING

In a small bowl:
  1 cup part-skim ricotta cheese
  6 tablespoons orange juice concentrate
  8 packets Equal® sweetener
Combine until smooth.

Place one cake on a serving plate. Spread with 1/2 cheese mixture. Place remaining cake on top and spread with remaining mixture. Decorate top of cake with 1/2 cup canned orange sections.

◆ STRAWBERRY MORNING CAKE ◆

2 cups fresh sliced strawberries
1/2 cup SugarTwin® brown sugar substitute
3/4 cup whole wheat flour
2/3 cup nonfat dry powdered milk
2 teaspoons baking soda
4 teaspoons cinnamon
1 1/2 tablespoons SugarTwin® brown sugar substitute
2 tablespoons plus 2 teaspoons reduced calorie vegetable oil
   margarine
1 cup part-skim ricotta cheese
1 tablespoon vanilla
1 teaspoon almond flavoring
1 1/2 tablespoons SugarTwin® brown sugar substitute

EXCHANGES

Each serving:
   1 protein exchange
   1 bread exchange
   1 fruit exchange
   1/2 milk exchange
   1 fat exchange

I just love cake for breakfast, don't you? When you can make it good for you, it's like having a sin forgiven!

In a small bowl:
  2 cups fresh strawberries, sliced
  1/2 cup SugarTwin® brown sugar substitute
  Combine and set aside.

In a large bowl:
  3/4 cup whole wheat flour
  2/3 cup nonfat dry powdered milk
  2 teaspoons baking soda
  4 teaspoons cinnamon
  1 1/2 tablespoons SugarTwin® brown sugar substitute
  2 tablespoons plus 2 teaspoons reduced calorie vegetable oil
    margarine, melted and cooled

Mix well.

In another bowl:
  1 cup part-skim ricotta cheese
  1 tablespoon vanilla
  1 teaspoon almond flavoring
  1 1/2 tablespoons SugarTwin® brown sugar substitute

Combine thoroughly and mix with 3/4 of the flour mixture. Press into an 8 x 8-inch baking dish sprayed with nonstick cooking spray. Top with strawberries. Sprinkle remaining 1/4 flour mixture on top of strawberries.

Bake at 350° for 30–45 minutes. Cool. Refrigerate overnight.

◆ BOTTOMS UP NECTARINE CAKE ◆

2 tablespoons reduced calorie vegetable oil margarine
1/4 cup SugarTwin® brown sugar substitute
4 small or 2 large ripe nectarines
1/4 cup reduced calorie vegetables oil margarine
1/2 cup SugarTwin® brown sugar substitute
2 eggs
1/2 cup skim milk
1 teaspoon vanilla
3/4 cup whole wheat flour
1 teaspoon baking powder
1/2 teaspoon salt

EXCHANGES

Each serving:

1/4 protein exchange
1/2 bread exchange
1/2 fruit exchange
1 fat exchange
11 extra calories

If we could only keep summer fruits around all year long.
Take advantage when you can.

In a small skillet:
   2 tablespoons reduced calorie vegetable oil margarine, melted over
      medium heat

Add: 1/4 cup SugarTwin® brown sugar substitute

Stir constantly for 2 minutes. Pour into a 8-inch round baking pan.
Spread evenly.

Prepare: 4 small or 2 large ripe nectarines, halved, pitted and thinly
      sliced

Arrange overlapping in circle in pan.

In a large bowl: 1/4 cup reduced calorie vegetables oil margarine

Beat with electric mixer until creamy.

Add: 1/2 cup SugarTwin® brown sugar substitute

Beat until light and fluffy.

Add: 2 eggs

Beat until blended.

Add:
   1/2 cup skim milk
   1 teaspoon vanilla
Mix until blended.

In a small bowl:
   3/4 cup whole wheat flour
   1 teaspoon baking powder
   1/2 teaspoon salt

Mix with whisk. Add to batter. Mix on low speed until blended.
Spread batter evenly over nectarines. Bake at 350° for 30-35 minutes,
until wooden pick comes out clean.

◆ GRANNY'S APPLE CAKE ◆
With Lemon Sauce

1 cup plus 2 tablespoons whole wheat flour
1/2 cup SugarTwin® brown sugar substitute
2 teaspoons baking powder
2 teaspoons cinnamon
1/2 teaspoon salt
3 eggs, beaten
2 teaspoons vanilla
1/4 cup reduced calorie vegetable oil margarine
3 small Granny Smith apples

LEMON SAUCE

1 1/2 cups plain low-fat yogurt
1 tablespoon lemon peel
6 packets Equal® sweetener

E X C H A N G E S

Each serving:
1/2 protein exchange
1 bread exchange
1/2 fruit exchange
1/2 milk exchange
1 fat exchange

*Treat your family like company with this wonderful cake and sauce.
Maybe they'll offer to do the dishes.*

In a large bowl:

> 1 cup plus 2 tablespoons whole wheat flour
> 1/2 cup SugarTwin® brown sugar substitute
> 2 teaspoons baking powder
> 2 teaspoons cinnamon
> 1/2 teaspoon salt

Mix well.

Add:

> 3 eggs, beaten
> 2 teaspoons vanilla
> 1/4 cup reduced calorie vegetable oil margarine, melted and
> cooled.

Mix thoroughly.

Fold in 3 small Granny Smith apples, peeled and chopped.

Spoon batter into an 8-inch round baking dish, sprayed with
nonstick cooking spray. Bake at 400° for 20 minutes or until wooden
pick comes out clean. Cool for 10 minutes then turn out on rack to
complete cooling.

LEMON SAUCE

> 1 1/2 cups plain low-fat yogurt
> 1 tablespoon lemon peel
> 6 packets Equal® sweetener

Mix and refrigerate until ready to use.

To serve, cut cake into 6 wedges and top evenly with lemon sauce.

◆ A SPECIAL CHEESECAKE ◆

4 graham crackers, 2 1/2 inches square
2 packets Equal® sweetener to remaining crumbs
1/3 cup reduced calorie vegetable oil margarine
1/4 cup SugarTwin® brown sugar substitute
1 1/2 cups part-skim ricotta cheese
1 cup plain low-fat yogurt
2 tablespoons lemon juice
1 tablespoon vanilla
1/2 teaspoon almond extract
2 egg yolks
1/4 cup plus 2 tablespoons whole wheat flour
1/4 teaspoon salt
2 egg whites
1/4 cup SugarTwin® brown sugar substitute

E X C H A N G E S

Each serving:
    1 protein exchange
    1/2 bread exchange
    1/4 milk exchange
    1 fat exchange

Not too rich, not too sweet. A great dessert anytime.

Better if made the day before.

Spray an 8-inch round baking dish with nonstick cooking spray.

Prepare: 4 graham crackers, 2 1/2 inches square

Crush with rolling pin until fine crumbs. Sprinkle 3/4 of the crumbs evenly on the bottom of the dish. Gently and lightly spray with cooking spray. Set aside.

Add: 2 packets Equal® sweetener to remaining crumbs

Mix well and set aside.

In a large bowl:
    1/3 cup reduced calorie vegetable oil margarine
    1/4 cup SugarTwin® brown sugar substitute

Beat with electric mixer until creamy.

Add:
    1 1/2 cup part-skim ricotta cheese
    1 cup plain low-fat yogurt
    Beat until smooth.

Add:
    2 tablespoons lemon juice
    1 tablespoon vanilla
    1/2 teaspoon almond
      extract
    2 egg yolks

Beat thoroughly.

Add:
    1/4 cup plus 2 tablespoons
      whole wheat flour
    1/4 teaspoon salt

Stir to combine.

In a small bowl:
    2 egg whites
    1/4 cup SugarTwin® brown
      sugar substitute

Beat until very soft peaks appear. Fold into cheese mixture. Pour into prepared baking dish. Bake at 350° for 35-45 minutes, until knife comes out clean. Sprinkle remaining crumbs evenly on top. Cool on rack. Refrigerate 10-12 hours or until ready to serve.

◆ FUDGE BROWNIE CAKE ◆

1/2 cup reduced calorie vegetable oil margarine
1 cup SugarTwin® brown sugar substitute
6 eggs
1 1/2 teaspoons vanilla
1 3/4 cups minus 1 tablespoon whole wheat flour
4 tablespoons cornstarch
1/3 cup unsweetened cocoa powder
1/2 teaspoon baking soda
1/4 cup boiling water

EXCHANGES

Each serving:
   1/2 protein exchange
   3/4 bread exchange
   1 fat exchange
   17 extra calories

Very dense but so good!!

In a large bowl:
  1/2 cup reduced calorie vegetable oil margarine

Beat with mixer on medium speed until smooth and creamy.

Add gradually: 1 cup SugarTwin® brown sugar substitute

Beat on low speed to incorporate, scrape bowl, then beat on high speed for 3 minutes.

Add: 6 eggs, room temperature, one at a time, beating thoroughly after each addition, scraping sides of bowl.

Add: 1 1/2 teaspoon vanilla

Stir to blend.

Combine: 1 3/4 cups minus 1 tablespoon whole wheat flour and 4 tablespoons cornstarch

Add to egg mixture in 3 additions, stirring until smooth.

In a small bowl:
  1/3 cup unsweetened cocoa powder
  1/2 teaspoon baking soda
  1/4 cup boiling water

Stir until smooth.

Add: 1 1/2 cups of the cake batter

Stir until blended.

Spoon remaining cake batter into a 9 x 5-inch loaf pan, sprayed with a nonstick cooking spray. Then spoon chocolate batter on top. Using a table knife cut through batters to create marbling. Bake at 325° in lower third of oven for 1 hour and 10 minutes or until wooden pick comes out clean. Cool in pan on rack for 10 minutes. Remove from pan and cool completely on rack, right side up.

◆ MAMA'S CARROT CAKE ◆
With Orange Sauce

1/2 cup raisins
1 cup water
3 cups grated carrots
4 eggs
1/4 cup SugarTwin® brown sugar substitute
2 tablespoons plus 2 teaspoons vegetable oil
1 teaspoon vanilla
1 1/2 cups whole wheat flour
1/4 cup dry buttermilk powder
1 teaspoon baking soda
1 teaspoon baking powder
2 teaspoons cinnamon

ORANGE SAUCE

2 cups plain low-fat yogurt
3 teaspoons orange extract
6 packets of Equal® sweetener

E X C H A N G E S

Each serving:
1/2 protein exchange
1 bread exchange
1/2 fruit exchange
3/4 milk exchange
1 fat exchange

Plumping the raisins and cooking the carrots is the secret to this moist cake.

In a small saucepan:
   1/2 cup raisins
   1 cup water

Bring to boil, cover and remove from heat. Set aside.When cool, drain and reserve 1/2 cup of the liquid.

In another saucepan with steamer:
   3 cups grated carrots
   Steam until completely cooked, cool.

In a large bowl:
   4 eggs
   1/4 cup SugarTwin® brown sugar substitute
   1/2 cup raisin liquid
   2 tablespoons plus 2 teaspoons vegetable oil
   1 teaspoon vanilla

Beat with electric mixer for 5 minutes.

In another bowl:
   1 1/2 cups whole wheat flour
   1/4 cup dry buttermilk powder
   1 teaspoon baking soda
   1 teaspoon baking powder
   2 teaspoons cinnamon

Mix well and add to egg mixture. Beat to combine thoroughly. If too stiff stir with large spoon.

Add drained carrots and raisins. Fold in and mix.

Pour into an 8-inch round or 8 x 8-inch baking dish, sprayed with nonstick cooking spray. Bake at 350° for 30–35 minutes or until wooden pick comes out clean. Cool for 10 minutes; then turn out on rack to complete cooling.

ORANGE SAUCE

   2 cups plain low-fat yogurt
   3 teaspoons orange extract
   6 packets of Equal® sweetener

To serve cut into 8 pieces and top evenly with orange sauce.

◆ GERMAN APPLE TORTE ◆

1/3 cup reduced calorie vegetable oil margarine
1/4 cup SugarTwin® brown sugar substitute
1 teaspoon vanilla
3/4 cup whole wheat flour
1 3/4 cups part-skim ricotta cheese
1/2 cup SugarTwin® brown sugar substitute
2 teaspoons lemon juice
1 teaspoon vanilla
4 small tart apples
1/4 cup SugarTwin® brown sugar substitute
1 teaspoon cinnamon

EXCHANGES

Each serving:
   1 protein exchange
   1/2 bread exchange
   1/2 fruit exchange
   1 fat exchange

Not just another apple recipe. A wonderfully different eating experience.

In a small bowl:

    1/3 cup reduced calorie vegetable oil margarine
    1/4 cup SugarTwin® brown sugar substitute
    1 teaspoon vanilla

Cream together.

Add: 3/4 cup whole wheat flour

Stir to blend. With fingers, press dough onto bottom and sides of a 9-inch pie pan.

In a medium-sized bowl:

    1 3/4 cups part-skim ricotta cheese
    1/2 cup SugarTwin® brown sugar substitute

Mix to combine.

Add:

    2 teaspoons lemon juice
    1 teaspoon vanilla

Blend to combine all ingredients. Pour into pastry-lined pie plate.

In a small bowl:

    4 small tart apples, peeled and sliced
    1/4 cup SugarTwin® brown sugar substitute
    1 teaspoon cinnamon

Mix together. Place apple slices on cheese mixture. Bake at 450° for 10 minutes; then reduce heat to 400° and bake 25 minutes longer or until knife comes out clean.

◆ A VERY SPECIAL BERRY TORTE ◆

3 tablespoons vegetable oil
5 packets Equal® sweetener
2 1/4 cups fresh strawberries
2 egg whites
4 packets Equal® sweetener
27 graham crackers, 2 1/2 inches square

EXCHANGES

Each serving:
    1 1/2 bread exchange
    1/2 fruit exchange
    1 fat exchange
    50 extra calories

Every once in a while, you've got to splurge. This is one of those times.

In a large bowl:
   3 tablespoons vegetable oil
   5 packets Equal® sweetener
   Stir to combine.

Add: 2 1/4 cups fresh strawberries, sliced

Stir together.

In a small bowl: 2 egg whites

Beat until soft peaks form.

Add: 4 packets Equal® sweetener

Continue to beat until stiff peaks form. Gently fold in strawberry mixture.

In an 8 x 8-inch baking dish arrange in single layer on bottom of dish: 9 graham crackers, 2 1/2 inches square

Spread one-half of strawberry mixture over crackers.

Top with: 9 graham crackers, 2 1/2 inches square

Spread remaining mixture over crackers.

Top with: 9 graham crackers, 2 1/2 inches square

Cover and refrigerate overnight.

To serve: Spread 1 tablespoon whipped cream atop each graham cracker square.

·2·

Cookies,
Bars
&
Brownies

◆ FUDGY COTTAGE COOKIES ◆

1/4 cup softened reduced calorie vegetable oil margarine
1/2 cup SugarTwin® brown sugar substitute
2/3 cup low-fat cottage cheese
1 egg
2 teaspoons vanilla
1 cup plus 2 tablespoons whole wheat flour
1 tablespoon unsweetened cocoa powder
1 teaspoon baking powder
1/2 teaspoon baking soda

EXCHANGES

Each serving Equals 5 cookies:
   1/2 protein exchange
   1 bread exchange
   1 fat exchange
   8 extra calories

Ummm—chocolate cookies and good for us, too!!

In a food processor or in a large bowl with an electric mixer:
- 1/4 cup softened reduced calorie vegetable oil margarine
- 1/2 cup SugarTwin® brown sugar substitute
- 2/3 cup low-fat cottage cheese
- 1 egg
- 2 teaspoons vanilla

Whirl or beat until smoothly blended.

In a medium-sized bowl:
- 1 cup plus 2 tablespoons whole wheat flour
- 1 tablespoon unsweetened cocoa powder
- 1 teaspoon baking powder
- 1/2 teaspoon baking soda

Stir with whisk to combine. Add to cheese mixture. Stir to blend. Refrigerate for 1 hour.

Remove dough from refrigerator and form 30 balls, spacing them about 1 1/2 inches apart on baking sheet sprayed with nonstick cooking spray. Bake at 350° about 12 minutes until cookies feel firm when touched. Cool on a rack.

◆ PEANUT BUTTER PUFFS ◆

2 1/2 cups whole wheat flour
1 cup nonfat dry powdered milk
1/2 cup SugarTwin® brown sugar substitute
2 tablespoons baking powder
3 eggs
1 cup water
3/4 cup chunky peanut butter

EXCHANGES

Each serving:
  1 1/4 protein exchange
  1 bread exchange
  1/4 milk exchange
  1 fat exchange

Everybody loves peanut butter cookies.

In a large bowl:
    2 1/2 cups whole wheat flour
    1 cup nonfat dry powdered milk
    1/2 cup SugarTwin® brown sugar substitute
    2 tablespoons baking powder
Stir with a whisk to combine.

Add:
    3 eggs, beaten
    1 cup water
Stir to combine.

Add: 3/4 cup chunky peanut butter

Stir to combine.

Drop by large spoonfuls on baking sheet. Bake at 400° for 12 minutes until lightly browned. Makes 48 cookies. Each serving is 4 cookies.

◆ APPLE PUMPKIN COOKIES ◆

2 small apples
1/2 cup canned pumpkin
3 tablespoons whole wheat flour
2/3 cup nonfat dry powdered milk
2 tablespoons SugarTwin® brown sugar substitute
1 teaspoon cinnamon
1/2 teaspoon nutmeg
1/2 teaspoon almond extract
1/2 teaspoon cinnamon
2 packets Equal® sweetener

E X C H A N G E S

Each serving:
    1/2 bread exchange
    1 fruit exchange
    1 milk exchange

Have some canned pumpkin left from another recipe?
Well, here's a quick and easy way to get another treat.

In a medium-sized bowl:

    2 small apples, cored, peeled, and grated
    1/2 cup canned pumpkin
    3 tablespoons whole wheat flour
    2/3 cup nonfat dry powdered milk
    2 tablespoons SugarTwin® brown sugar substitute
    1 teaspoon cinnamon
    1/2 teaspoon nutmeg
    1/2 teaspoon almond extract

Mix until thoroughly combined. Spoon into 8 mounds on baking
sheet, sprayed with nonstick cooking spray. Flatten with a spoon.
Bake at 375° for 20 minutes.

In a small bowl:

    1/2 teaspoon cinnamon
    2 packets Equal® sweetener

Combine and sprinkle on cookies as soon as removed from oven.
Cool cookies on rack.

◆ RAISIN OATMEAL COOKIES ◆

2 cups raisins
1 cup water
1/2 cup vegetable oil
1/3 cup reduced calorie vegetable oil margarine
2 cups SugarTwin® brown sugar substitute
3 eggs
1 tablespoon vanilla
1/4 cup skim milk
2 1/4 cups whole wheat flour
5 cups quick-cooking rolled oats
2 teaspoons baking powder
1 teaspoon cream of tartar
1 teaspoon cinnamon

E X C H A N G E S

Each serving:
1 bread exchange
1 fat exchange
1/2 fruit exchange
8 extra calories

An old favorite. So good to have on hand.

In a saucepan:
    2 cups raisins
    1 cup water
Bring to a boil. Cover and remove from heat. Set aside.

In a large bowl:
    1/2 cup vegetable oil
    1/3 cup reduced calorie vegetable oil margarine
Beat with electric mixer until creamy.

Add: 2 cups SugarTwin® brown sugar substitute

Beat until blended.

Add:
    3 eggs
    1 tablespoon vanilla
    1/4 cup skim milk
Beat until blended.

In another large bowl:
    2 1/4 cups whole wheat flour
    5 cups quick-cooking rolled oats
    2 teaspoons baking powder
    1 teaspoon cream of tartar
    1 teaspoon cinnamon
Mix with a whisk. Add to egg mixture. Stir until moist.

Add: Raisins with any water still remaining . Stir to blend.

Chill batter in refrigerator 15–20 minutes. Using an ice cream scoop, make 32 huge cookies, then press flat. Bake at 375° for 15 minutes or until firm to touch. Use upper third of oven.

◆ CHEESY STRAWBERRY PUFFS ◆

2 tablespoons reduced calorie vegetable oil margarine
2 eggs
1/2 cup plus 1 tablespoon whole wheat flour
1/2 cup skim milk
1/2 teaspoon part-skim milk ricotta cheese
1 teaspoon strawberry or other favorite sugar-free jam

E X C H A N G E S

Each serving:
   1/2 protein exchange
   1/2 bread exchange
   1/2 fat exchange
   16 extra calories

Don't miss out on this 2–step delicious mouth–happy treat.

In a 12-cup (2–2 1/2 inch) muffin pan: 2 tablespoons reduced calorie vegetable oil margarine divided evenly

Set in 425° oven to melt, about 3 minutes.

In a food processor or blender jar:
  2 eggs
  1/2 cup plus 1 tablespoon whole wheat flour
  1/2 cup skim milk
Whirl to blend.

Spoon 2 tablespoons batter into each muffin cup.
Bake about 3–4 minutes.

Remove from oven and quickly add to each cup:
  1/2 teaspoon part-skim milk ricotta cheese
  1 teaspoon strawberry or other favorite sugar-free jam

Continue to bake until puffed and browned on edges, about 10 more minutes. Cool slightly in pan on rack. Scoop out with large spoon. Serve warm or at room temperature.

Two puffs equal 1 serving.

◆ CHEWY BROWNIES ◆

3/4 cup whole wheat flour
1/4 teaspoon baking soda
1/4 teaspoon salt
1/3 cup reduced calorie vegetable oil margarine
2 tablespoons water
3/4 cup SugarTwin® brown sugar substitute
1/4 cup unsweetened cocoa powder
1/2 cup skim milk
1 teaspoon vanilla
1/2 teaspoon almond extract
2 eggs

EXCHANGES

Each serving:
  1/4 protein exchange
  1 fat exchange
  1/2 bread exchange
  13 extra calories

A little less sweet but chocolate and chewy just the same.
Give it a try; you'll find it a treat!

In a small bowl:
    3/4 cup whole wheat flour
    1/4 teaspoon baking soda
    1/4 teaspoon salt

Combine with a whisk.

In a 2-quart saucepan:
    1/3 cup reduced calorie vegetable oil margarine
    2 tablespoons water

Bring to a boil, stirring with a whisk until margarine is completely melted. Remove from heat.

Add:
    3/4 cup SugarTwin® brown sugar substitute
    1/4 cup unsweetened cocoa powder

Whisk until stiff.

Add:
    1/2 cup skim milk
    1 teaspoon vanilla
    1/2 teaspoon almond extract

Whisk until smooth.

Add: 2 eggs
Whisk in one at a time.

Add: Flour mixture

Stir to combine all ingredients. Pour into a 8 x 8-inch baking dish, sprayed with nonstick cooking spray. Bake at 350° for 35–40 minutes. Cool on a rack.

◆ APRICOT BARS ◆

32 dried apricot halves
1 cup water
1/2 cup SugarTwin® brown sugar substitute
1 tablespoon cornstarch dissolved in 1/2 cup water
1/2 teaspoon ground coriander
1 teaspoon vanilla
1/2 cup plus 1 tablespoon whole wheat flour
1/2 cup quick-cooking rolled oats
1/2 cup 100% whole bran cereal
1/3 cup reduced calorie vegetable oil margarine

EXCHANGES

Each serving:
    3/4 bread exchange
    1 fruit exchange
    1 fat exchange

With all the dried apricot recipes in this book, you have probably guessed they are my favorite dried fruit. You're right.

In a saucepan:
>32 dried apricot halves, cut into 1/4 inch pieces
>1 cup water

Bring to a boil. Cover and simmer 20-25 minutes.

Add:
>1/2 cup SugarTwin® brown sugar substitute
>1 tablespoon cornstarch dissolved in 1/2 cup water
>1/2 teaspoon ground coriander

Stir and cook until thickened. Remove from heat.

Add: 1 teaspoon vanilla

Stir to blend.

In a medium size bowl:
>1/2 cup plus 1 tablespoon whole wheat flour
>1/2 cup quick-cooking rolled oats
>1/2 cup 100% whole bran cereal

Mix with a whisk.

Add: 1/3 cup reduced calorie vegetable oil margarine

Cut in until mixture is crumbly. Set aside 1/2 cup of crumb mixture. Stir 1/4 cup water into remaining crumbs. Press mixture in bottom of 8 x 8-inch baking dish. Top with apricot mixture, then reserved crumbs, and press lightly. Bake at 350° for 30–35 minutes. Cool on rack. Cut in half and then in four, giving a total of 8 bars.

◆ CHEWY DESSERT BARS ◆

1 cup plus 2 tablespoons whole wheat flour
1/2 teaspoon baking powder
1/2 cup reduced calorie vegetable oil margarine
3/4 cup SugarTwin® brown sugar substitute
24 dried apricots halves
18 pitted prunes

EXCHANGES

Each serving:
  1/2 bread exchange
  1 fruit exchange
  1 fat exchange
  6 extra calories

Dried fruit is so wonderful. Here are two favorites together in this great dessert.

In a small bowl:
  1 cup plus 2 tablespoons whole wheat flour
  1/2 teaspoon baking powder

Mix with a whisk.

In a large bowl:
  1/2 cup reduced calorie vegetable oil margarine at room
    temperature
  3/4 cup SugarTwin® brown sugar substitute

Beat with electric mixer until fluffy.

Add: 1 egg

Beat again. Stir in flour mixture until blended.

Add:
  24 dried apricots halves, cut into 1/4 inch pieces
  18 pitted prunes, cut in 1/4 inch pieces

Stir to blend. Spread evenly in a 12 x 8-inch baking dish, sprayed with nonstick cooking spray. Bake at 350° for 25 minutes or until top is lightly browned and edges pull away from sides of dish. Cool in pan on rack. Cut lengthwise and then into sixes, making 12 bars.

◆ SPICY ZUCCHINI BARS ◆

1 3/4 cups minus 1 tablespoon whole wheat flour
1 1/2 teaspoons baking powder
1 1/2 teaspoons cinnamon
1/2 teaspoon nutmeg
3/4 cup reduced calorie vegetable oil margarine
3/4 cup SugarTwin® brown sugar substitute
2 eggs
1 teaspoon vanilla
2 cups zucchini

E X C H A N G E S

Each serving:
   1/2 bread exchange
   1 fat exchange
   8 extra calories

What a great vegetable to make such a lot of wonderful treats, this being one of them.

In a small bowl:
   1 3/4 cups minus 1 tablespoon whole wheat flour
   1 1/2 teaspoons baking powder
   1 1/2 teaspoons cinnamon
   1/2 teaspoon nutmeg

Mix with a whisk.

In a large bowl:
   3/4 cup reduced calorie vegetable oil margarine

Beat with electric mixer until creamy.

Add: 3/4 cup SugarTwin® brown sugar substitute

Beat until fluffy.

Add:
   2 eggs
   1 teaspoon vanilla

Beat until blended.

Stir in flour mixture.

Add: 2 cups zucchini, shredded

Stir to thoroughly combine. Spread into a 13 x 8-inch baking dish, sprayed with nonstick cooking spray. Bake at 350° for 30 minutes or until wooden pick comes out clean. Cool on rack. Cut into 18 bars.

◆ SAUCY RAISIN APPLE BARS ◆

1/4 cup plus 2 tablespoons raisins
1 1/2 cups whole wheat flour
1 teaspoon cinnamon
1 teaspoon baking powder
1/2 teaspoon baking soda
1/4 teaspoon ground cloves
1/3 cup reduced calorie vegetable oil margarine
1/2 cup SugarTwin® brown sugar substitute
1 large egg
1 cup unsweetened apple sauce
3 small golden delicious apples
raisins
water

EXCHANGES

Each serving:
    1 bread exchange
    1 fruit exchange
    1 fat exchange
    9 extra calories

Great for lunch boxes or take along on a picnic.

In a small saucepan:

  1/4 cup plus 2 tablespoons raisins covered with water

Bring to a boil, cover and remove from heat. After 15 minutes, drain and set aside.

In a large bowl:

  1 1/2 cups whole wheat flour
  1 teaspoon cinnamon
  1 teaspoon baking powder
  1/2 teaspoon baking soda
  1/4 teaspoon ground cloves

Mix well.

In another bowl:

  1/3 cup reduced calorie vegetable oil margarine at room
    temperature
  1/2 cup SugarTwin® brown sugar substitute

Cream.

Add:

  1 large egg
  1 cup unsweetened apple sauce

Mix with a whisk and add to flour mixture. Mix to combine thoroughly.

Fold in:

3 small golden delicious apples, peeled and diced

raisins, drained

Spread in a 12 x 8-inch baking dish, sprayed with nonstick cooking spray. Bake at 375° for 45 minutes. Cool in dish.

·3·

Dessert
Breads
&
Coffee
Cakes

◆ UP COUNTRY APPLE BREAD ◆

1/2 cup raisins
2 eggs
1/2 cup SugarTwin® brown sugar substitute
2/3 cup unsweetened apple juice
1/3 cup reduced calorie mayonnaise
1/2 teaspoon vanilla
1 1/2 cups whole wheat flour
1/4 cup dry buttermilk powder
1/8 teaspoon salt
1 teaspoon baking powder
1/2 teaspoon baking soda
1 teaspoon cinnamon
2 small tart green apples
water

EXCHANGES

Each serving:

1/4 protein exchange
1 bread exchange
1 fruit exchange
1/4 milk exchange
1 fat exchange

This bread is good anytime. Makes a quick take-along breakfast.
Keep a bread in the freezer in case someone drops in. If they don't,
maybe you'll have to eat it yourself.

In a small saucepan:
> 1/2 cup raisins, covered with water
> Bring to boil, cover and remove from heat. After 15 minutes,
>   drain and set aside.

In a large bowl:
> 2 eggs
> 1/2 cup SugarTwin® brown sugar substitute
> 2/3 cup unsweetened apple juice
> 1/3 cup reduced calorie mayonnaise
> 1/2 teaspoon vanilla

Beat with a whisk until smooth.

In another bowl:
> 1 1/2 cups whole wheat flour
> 1/4 cup dry buttermilk powder
> 1/8 teaspoon salt
> 1 teaspoon baking powder
> 1/2 teaspoon baking soda
> 1 teaspoon cinnamon

Mix well. Add to egg mixture and stir to mix thoroughly.

Add: 2 small tart green apples, cored and chopped.
> Leave peeling on.

> Raisins, drained

Mix to combine.

Spread in a 9 x 5-inch loaf pan, sprayed with nonstick cooking spray.
Bake at 375° for 50 minutes or until wooden pick comes out clean.
Cool in pan for 10 minutes. Turn out on rack to cool bottom.

◆ DOUBLE "O" BREAD ◆

3 small oranges
2 teaspoons grated orange peel
1 3/4 cups minus 1 tablespoon whole wheat flour
3/4 cup quick-cooking oats
3/4 cup SugarTwin® brown sugar substitute
2 teaspoons baking powder
1 teaspoon salt
orange peel
1 3/4 cups minus 1 tablespoon whole wheat flour
3/4 cup quick-cooking oats
3/4 cup SugarTwin® brown sugar substitute
2 teaspoons baking powder
1 teaspoon salt
orange peel
1 large egg, beaten
1 1/2 cups buttermilk
1/4 cup vegetable oil

EXCHANGES

Each serving:
 1 bread exchange
 1/4 fruit exchange
 1 fat exchange
 21 extra calories

Great for breakfast or freeze for that little something when company drops in.

From an orange, grate 2 teaspoons peel. Peel and seed 3 small oranges; cut into 1-inch pieces and puree in blender.

In a large bowl:

1 3/4 cups minus 1 tablespoon whole wheat flour
3/4 cup quick-cooking oats, uncooked
3/4 cup SugarTwin® brown sugar substitute
2 teaspoons baking powder
1 teaspoon salt
orange peel

Mix with a whisk to combine.

In a small bowl:

1 large egg, beaten
1 1/2 cups buttermilk
1/4 cup vegetable oil
orange puree

Stir to combine. Add to flour mixture. Stir to moisten all ingredients. Pack batter firmly into an 8 1/2 x 4 1/2-inch loaf pan which has been sprayed with a nonstick spraying agent. Bake at 350° for 50–60 minutes until wooden pick comes out clean. Cool in pan on rack 10 minutes. Remove from pan and cool completely on rack.

◆ HOLIDAY PUMPKIN BREAD ◆

1 cup raisins
1 cup water
2 eggs
1/2 cup SugarTwin® brown sugar substitute
2 tablespoons plus 2 teaspoons vegetable oil
1 cup canned pumpkin
1 1/2 cups whole wheat flour
2/3 cup nonfat dry powdered milk
1 teaspoon baking soda
1 teaspoon baking powder
1 teaspoon pumpkin pie spice
1/2 teaspoon cinnamon

EXCHANGES

Each serving:
1/4 protein exchange
1 bread exchange
1 fruit exchange
1/4 milk exchange
1 fat exchange

Don't wait for the holidays to make this. Serve it tonight.

In a small saucepan:
    1 cup raisins
    1 cup water

Bring to boil, cover and remove from heat. Set aside. When cool, drain.

In a large bowl:
    2 eggs
    1/2 cup SugarTwin® brown sugar substitute
    2 tablespoons plus 2 teaspoons vegetable oil

Beat with electric mixer for 1 minute.

Add: 1 cup canned pumpkin

Beat to mix.

In another bowl:
    1 1/2 cups whole wheat flour
    2/3 cup nonfat dry powdered milk
    1 teaspoon baking soda
    1 teaspoon baking powder
    1 teaspoon pumpkin pie spice
    1/2 teaspoon cinnamon

Mix well and add to egg mixture. Beat to combine thoroughly. Fold in raisins, drained. Pour into a 9 x 5-inch loaf pan, sprayed with nonstick cooking spray. Bake at 350° for 35 – 40 minutes or until wooden pick comes out clean. Cool in pan for 10 minutes, then turn out on rack to cool bottom.

◆ CHEESY APPLE BREAD ◆

1 1/2 cups whole wheat flour
1/3 cup SugarTwin® brown sugar substitute
2/3 cup nonfat dry powdered milk
1 tablespoon baking powder
1 teaspoon cinnamon
1/2 teaspoon salt
2 eggs, beaten
2/3 cup unsweetened apple juice
5 tablespoons plus 1 teaspoon reduced calorie vegetable oil
    margarine
6 oz. cheddar cheese, shredded
2 small apples

EXCHANGES

Each serving:
    1 protein exchange
    1 bread exchange
    1/2 fruit exchange
    1 fat exchange

A good old American tradition—apples with cheese in a great bread.

In a large bowl:
    1 1/2 cups whole wheat flour
    1/3 cup SugarTwin® brown sugar substitute
    2/3 cup nonfat dry powdered milk
    1 tablespoon baking powder
    1 teaspoon cinnamon
    1/2 teaspoon salt

Mix well.

In another bowl:
    2 eggs, beaten
    2/3 cup unsweetened apple juice
    5 tablespoons plus 1 teaspoon reduced calorie vegetable oil
        margarine, melted and cooled

Combine with a whisk and add to flour mixture.

Fold in:
    6 oz. cheddar cheese, shredded
    2 small apples, peeled, cored and chopped

Spoon batter into a 9 x 5-inch loaf pan sprayed with nonstick cooking spray. Bake at 350° for 1 hour and 15 minutes. Test with wooden pick after 1 hour. When pick comes out clean, remove from oven. Cool in pan on rack for 10 minutes, then turn out on rack to cool bottom.

◆ CRANBERRY DATE BREAD ◆

1 1/2 cups plus 3 tablespoons whole wheat flour
1 1/2 teaspoon baking powder
1/2 teaspoon salt
3/4 cup SugarTwin® brown sugar substitute
1 egg
12 teaspoons reduced calorie vegetable oil margarine
1/2 cup unsweetened orange juice
2 tablespoons hot water
1 cup fresh cranberries
6 pitted dates
1 tablespoon grated orange peel

EXCHANGES

Each serving:
   3/4 bread exchange
   1/2 fruit exchange
   1/2 fat exchange
   6 extra calories

Perfect for the holiday. Make several and freeze for all your holiday needs.

In a large bowl:

  1 1/2 cups plus 3 tablespoons whole wheat flour
  1 1/2 teaspoon baking powder
  1/2 teaspoon salt
  3/4 cup SugarTwin® brown sugar substitute

Stir with a whisk to mix.

Add:

  1 egg, beaten
  12 teaspoons reduced calorie vegetable oil margarine
  1/2 cup unsweetened orange juice
  2 tablespoons hot water

Stir until just moistened.

Add:

  1 cup fresh cranberries, coarsely chopped
  6 pitted dates, chopped
  1 tablespoon grated orange peel

Fold in to blend.

Spoon into a 9 x 5-inch loaf pan, sprayed with nonstick cooking spray. Bake at 350° for 45–55 minutes or until wooden pick comes out clean. Cool on rack for 10 minutes; then remove from pan and invert on rack to finish cooling.

◆ KIWI TEA BREAD ◆

8 medium-sized firm-ripe kiwi fruit
3/4 cup SugarTwin® brown sugar substitute
1 teaspoon grated lemon peel
2 eggs
1/3 cup reduced calorie vegetable oil margarine
1/2 teaspoon baking soda
1 1/2 cups whole wheat flour
1 teaspoon baking powder
1/2 teaspoon salt

E X C H A N G E S

Each serving:

    1/4 protein exchange
    1 bread exchange
    1 fruit exchange
    1 fat exchange

A wonderful tropical fruit in a new experience.

In a 2-quart pan:
   8 medium-sized firm-ripe kiwi fruit, pared and chopped
   (Chop enough fruit to make 1 1/2 cups; slice remaining
   fruit, wrap in plastic, refrigerate for garnish)
   3/4 cup SugarTwin® brown sugar substitute
   1 teaspoon grated lemon peel

Bring to a boil, stirring; cook until fruit pales in color. Remove from
heat and let cool.

Stir with a whisk to mix.

In a large bowl:
   2 eggs
   1/3 cup reduced calorie vegetable oil margarine

Beat until well mixed.

Add: 1/2 teaspoon baking soda
Stir until small bubbles appear. Add to egg mixture.

In a small bowl:
   1 1/2 cups whole wheat flour
   1 teaspoon baking powder
   1/2 teaspoon salt

Stir with a whisk to mix. Add to egg mixture. Stir until all
ingredients are moistened. Spoon into a 9 x 5-inch loaf pan, sprayed
with nonstick cooking spray. Bake at 350° for 50–55 minutes until
wooden pick comes out clean. Cool on rack for 10 minutes and then
invert on rack to finish cooling. Refrigerate until ready to serve.
Garnish with reserved fruit slices.

◆ PLUM GOOD COFFEECAKE ◆

1 cup plus 2 tablespoons whole wheat flour
1/2 cup SugarTwin® brown sugar substitute
2 teaspoons baking powder
1 teaspoon cinnamon
1/2 teaspoon nutmeg
3 eggs
3/4 cup buttermilk
1/4 cup reduced calorie vegetable oil margarine
6 medium plums
1/2 teaspoon cinnamon
2 tablespoons SugarTwin® brown sugar substitute

EXCHANGES

Each serving:
    1/2 protein exchange
    1 bread exchange
    1/2 fruit exchange
    1 fat exchange
    15 extra calories

Take advantage of the summer fruit and delight your family with this on Sunday morning.

In a large bowl:
  1 cup plus 2 tablespoons whole wheat flour
  1/2 cup SugarTwin® brown sugar substitute
  2 teaspoons baking powder
  1 teaspoon cinnamon
  1/2 teaspoon nutmeg

Stir with whisk to combine.

In a small bowl:
  3 eggs, beaten
  3/4 cup buttermilk
  1/4 cup reduced calorie vegetable oil margarine, melted and
    cooled

Stir until blended. Add to flour mixture. Stir to combine completely. Spread into a 9-inch round cake pan, sprayed with nonstick cooking spray.

Prepare: 6 medium plums, cut in half

Place plum halves cut side up on top of cake batter; press slightly into batter.

Combine:
  1/2 teaspoon cinnamon
  2 tablespoons SugarTwin® brown sugar substitute

Sprinkle on top of fruit and batter. Bake at 375° for 40 – 45 minutes until well browned.

◆ SPICY COFFEECAKE ◆

3/4 cup SugarTwin® brown sugar substitute
1/8 teaspoon salt
1 teaspoon vanilla
3 eggs
2 teaspoons instant coffee granules
1/2 cup boiling water
2 tablespoons reduced calorie vegetable oil margarine
1 cup plus 1 tablespoon whole wheat flour
2 teaspoons baking powder
1 teaspoon cinnamon
1 teaspoon nutmeg
1/2 teaspoon ginger
1/2 teaspoon allspice

E X C H A N G E S

Each serving:
    1/2 protein exchange
    1 bread exchange
    1/2 fat exchange

Truly a well named cake.

In a large bowl:
   3/4 cup SugarTwin® brown sugar substitute
   1/8 teaspoon salt
   1 teaspoon vanilla
   3 eggs

Beat with mixer at high speed for 5 minutes.

In a small saucepan:
   2 teaspoons instant coffee granules
   1/2 cup boiling water
   2 tablespoons reduced calorie vegetable oil margarine

Bring to a boil stirring until margarine is melted.

Add to sugar mixture and beat a low speed until well blended.

Add:
   1 cup plus 1 tablespoon whole wheat flour
   2 teaspoons baking powder
   1 teaspoon cinnamon
   1 teaspoon nutmeg
   1/2 teaspoon ginger
   1/2 teaspoon allspice

Beat at medium speed until well blended and smooth.

Pour into 8 x 8-inch baking dish, sprayed with nonstick cooking spray and dusted with 1 tablespoon whole wheat flour.
Bake at 350° for 20 minutes. Cool completely in pan on rack.

·4·

Pies
&
Tarts

◆ EASY PUMPKIN PIE ◆

3 eggs
1/2 cup plus 1 tablespoon whole wheat flour
2 tablespoons reduced calorie vegetable oil margarine
12 ounces canned evaporated skim milk
16 ounces canned pumpkin
1/2 cup SugarTwin® brown sugar substitute
1 teaspoon baking powder
2 1/2 teaspoons pumpkin pie spice
2 teaspoon vanilla

E X C H A N G E S

Each serving:
> 1/2 protein exchange
> 1/2 bread exchange
> 1/2 milk exchange
> 1/2 fat exchange

As it says, easy one-step process and there you have it, a pumpkin pie as often as you have a taste for one.

In a blender jar:
3 eggs
1/2 cup plus 1 tablespoon whole wheat flour
2 tablespoons reduced calorie vegetable oil margarine, melted
12 ounces canned evaporated skim milk
16 ounces canned pumpkin
1/2 cup SugarTwin® brown sugar substitute
1 teaspoon baking powder
2 1/2 teaspoons pumpkin pie spice
2 teaspoons vanilla

Blend on high speed for 1 minute. Pour into 9 or 10-inch pie plate, sprayed with nonstick cooking spray.

Bake at 350° for 50–55 minutes until knife comes out clean.

◆ IMPOSSIBLE CHEESE PIE ◆

4 eggs
1 cup part-skim ricotta cheese
1/2 cup SugarTwin® brown sugar substitute
2 cups skim milk
1/4 cup plus 2 tablespoons whole wheat flour
2 tablespoons reduced calorie vegetable oil margarine
1 tablespoon lemon extract
1 tablespoon vanilla extract
4 cups unsweetened fresh or frozen raspberries
8 packets Equal® sweetener

EXCHANGES

Each serving:
    1 protein exchange
    1/4 bread exchange
    1/4 milk exchange
    3/4 fat exchange
    8 extra calories

This one-step process makes you one step away from a deliciously different dessert.

In a blender jar, in the following order:
4 eggs
1 cup part-skim ricotta cheese
1/2 cup SugarTwin® brown sugar substitute
2 cups skim milk
1/4 cup plus 2 tablespoons whole wheat flour
2 tablespoons reduced calorie vegetable oil margarine, melted
1 tablespoon lemon extract
1 tablespoon vanilla extract

Whirl on high until well blended. Pour into a 9-inch pie pan, sprayed with nonstick cooking spray. Bake at 350° for 40–45 minutes or until knife comes out clean. Cool on rack and then refrigerate until ready to serve.

In a medium size bowl:
4 cups unsweetened fresh or frozen raspberries
8 packets Equal® sweetener

Mix and refrigerate. Divide evenly on cheese pie when serving.

◆ PEACHY CHIFFON PIE ◆

16 graham crackers, 2 1/2 inches square
2 tablespoons reduced calorie vegetable oil margarine
1 envelope unflavored gelatin
1/3 cup cold water
2 medium-sized fresh peaches
2 cups plain low-fat yogurt
4 packets Equal® sweetener
2 medium fresh peaches
2 eggs whites
8 packets Equal® sweetener

E X C H A N G E S

Each serving:
1 bread exchange
1/2 fruit exchange
1/2 milk exchange
1/2 fat exchange
5 extra calories

Cool and delightful on a warm summer day. Enjoy!

Prepare:
  16 graham crackers, 2 1/2-inches square

Crush with rolling pin until fine crumbs.

Add: 2 tablespoons reduced calorie vegetable oil margarine

Mix with fork or hands until completely combined. Press into an 8 or 9-inch pie plate, including sides. Bake at 375° for 5 minutes or until lightly browned. Set aside.

In a small saucepan:
  1 envelope unflavored gelatin
  1/3 cup cold water

Cook and stir until gelatin dissolves. Remove from heat.

Add:
  2 medium-sized fresh peaches, peeled and pureed
  2 cups plain low-fat yogurt
  4 packets Equal® sweetener

Stir to combine. Chill until partially set.

Add: 2 medium-sized fresh peaches, peeled and chopped

Fold in to combine.

In a large bowl: 2 eggs whites

Beat until soft peaks appear.

Add: 8 packets Equal® sweetener

Adding two packets at a time, beat until stiff peaks form. Fold in yogurt mixture. Turn into pie shell. Chill 3 to 4 hours or until ready to serve.

◆ PUMPKIN CHEESE DESSERT ◆

16 graham crackers, 2 1/2 inches square
1/3 cup reduced calorie vegetable oil margarine
1 cup part-skim ricotta cheese
1 1/2 cups canned pumpkin
2 eggs, slightly beaten
1/3 cup SugarTwin® brown sugar substitute
1 teaspoon cinnamon
1 teaspoon pumpkin pie spice
1 teaspoon vanilla

EXCHANGES

Each serving:

3/4 protein exchange
1 bread exchange
1 fat exchange

A wonderful pie for a special dessert.

In a food processor or blender:
   16 graham crackers, 2 1/2 inches square

Whirl until fine crumbs. Remove to a small bowl.

Add: 1/3 cup reduced calorie vegetable oil margarine

Mix until crumbs and margarine thoroughly combined. Press into a 9-inch pie plate including sides to the top of plate. Bake at 300° until crust feels firm about 25–35 minutes. Set aside.

In a medium-sized bowl:
   1 cup part-skim ricotta cheese
   1 1/2 cups canned pumpkin
   2 eggs, slightly beaten
   1/3 cup SugarTwin® brown sugar substitute
   1 teaspoon cinnamon
   1 teaspoon pumpkin pie spice
   1 teaspoon vanilla

Beat with electric mixer or whisk until smooth. Pour into baked crust. Bake at 350° for 30–40 minutes or until a knife comes out clean. Cool on rack; then refrigerate for at least one hour or until ready to serve.

◆ APPLE TARTS ◆

4 small green apples
1/2 teaspoon lemon peel
1 tablespoon lemon juice
1/2 teaspoon cinnamon
1/4 cup SugarTwin® brown sugar substitute
2 teaspoons reduced calorie vegetable margarine
1 cup whole wheat pastry flour
1/2 teaspoon salt
1/3 cup reduced calorie vegetable oil margarine

EXCHANGES

Each serves:
    1 bread exchange
    1 fruit exchange
    1 fat exchange
    10 extra calories

Whole wheat flour doesn't make as flaky a pie crust, but give it a try to see if you like the difference.

Prepare pastry dough (see below). Use half the dough for this recipe. Refrigerate or freeze remaining half or find the "Blueberry Treats" recipe in this book and double your pleasure.

In a medium-sized bowl:
- 4 small green apples, peeled, cored and sliced
- 1/2 teaspoon lemon peel
- 1 tablespoon lemon juice
- 1/2 teaspoon cinnamon
- 1/4 cup SugarTwin® brown sugar substitute

Mix well. Pour into pastry.

Equally dot with:
- 2 teaspoons reduced calorie vegetable margarine

Sprinkle top of apples with 1/2 teaspoon cinnamon equally distributed over all flour tarts.

Bake at 425° for 10–12 minutes.

PASTRY DOUGH

In a medium bowl:
- 1 cup whole wheat pastry flour
- 1/2 teaspoon salt

Mix with whisk.

Add: 1/3 cup reduced calorie vegetable oil margarine

With a pastry blender or 2 knives (scissor style) cut in margarine until mixture looks like coarse meal. Sprinkle 1 tablespoon cold water over part of the mixture; gently toss with a fork. Push to side of bowl. Repeat until all the mixture is moistened using 3-4 tablespoon cold water total. Gather dough into a rough ball. Refrigerate 20–30 minutes.

Put aside 2 tablespoons whole wheat pastry flour. Use to flour work surface and rolling pin. This recipe will make 8 small circles. Make each circle big enough to fit a small 6-ounce custard baking dish. Flute edges and prick with fork.

◆ BLUEBERRY TREATS ◆

Make pastry dough (see recipe "Apple Tarts" in this book).
    2 cups fresh blueberries
    1/2 cup water
    2 teaspoons lemon juice
    1/4 teaspoon cinnamon
    1 tablespoon cornstarch mixed with 1/2 cup water
    4 packets Equal® sweetener

————————— E X C H A N G E S —————————

Each serving:
        1 bread exchange
        1 fruit exchange
        1 fat exchange
        8 extra calories

Blueberries are my favorite. If they're yours too, no excuse not to make these often. After summer is gone, use unsweetened frozen berries.

Make pastry dough (see recipe "Apple Tarts" in this book).

Use 4 circles. Place in small custard baking dishes. Flute edges and prick entire dish with fork, bottom, sides and edges. Bake at 425° for 10 minutes or until lightly browned. Cool on rack.

In a saucepan:

    2 cups fresh blueberries
    1/2 cup water
    2 teaspoons lemon juice
    1/4 teaspoon cinnamon

Bring to a boil, then simmer until berries are soft.

Add: 1 tablespoon cornstarch mixed with 1/2 cup water

Stir until thickened. Remove from heat.

Stir in: 4 packets Equal® sweetener

Remove pastry shells from dishes and pour in mixture.
Ready to eat.

·5·

Puddings
&
Cobblers

◆ SPECIAL BREAD PUDDING ◆
FOR APRICOTS

8 slices wheat berry bread
1/2 cup raisins
4 medium-sized fresh apricots
1 teaspoon cinnamon, sprinkled on top
1 cup skim milk
1/2 cup SugarTwin® brown sugar substitute
1/2 teaspoon almond extract
4 eggs

EXCHANGES

Each serving:

    1/2 protein exchange
    1 bread exchange
    3/4 fruit exchange
    12 extra calories

Whether a dessert for a chilly winter night or reheated for a hearty warm breakfast, this one's a must! Served out of the refrigerator, it's good anytime.

In a large bowl:

　　8 slices wheatberry bread, cut into 1-inch squares
　　1/2 cup raisins
　　2 medium-sized fresh apricots cut into 1/2 inch chunks (if canned, use water packed or sugar-free)
　　1 teaspoon cinnamon, sprinkled on top

Mix to combine.

Place in an 8 x 8-inch baking dish sprayed with nonstick cooking spray.

In a large bowl:

　　2 medium-sized fresh apricots, mashed
　　1 cup skim milk
　　1/2 cup SugarTwin® brown sugar substitute
　　1/2 teaspoon almond extract
　　4 eggs

Beat with a whisk until blended. Pour over bread mixture. Press down on bread cubes until all are submerged. Place baking dish in large roasting pan on oven rack. Pour in boiling water until it is halfway up sides of baking dish.

Bake at 325° for 1 hour and 20 minutes or until knife in center comes out clean.

◆ GRANDMA'S RICE PUDDING ◆

4 eggs
1 1/2 cups evaporated skim milk
1 package vanilla flavored low-calorie milk beverage
2 teaspoon cinnamon
1/2 teaspoon vanilla
Dash nutmeg
3 teaspoons reduced calorie vegetable oil margarine
2 tablespoons SugarTwin® brown sugar substitute
2 cups cooked rice

EXCHANGES

Each serving:

　　1 protein exchange
　　1 bread exchange
　　1 milk exchange
　　1 fat exchange

Good anytime. Make the night before and warm for the next day's breakfast. So wonderful, you'll plan often to have leftover rice.

In a bowl:

    4 eggs, beaten
    1 1/2 cups evaporated skim milk
    1 package vanilla flavored low-calorie milk beverage

Beat with a whisk until smooth.

Add:

    2 teaspoon cinnamon
    1/2 teaspoon vanilla
    dash nutmeg
    3 teaspoons reduced calorie vegetable oil margarine, melted over low heat
    2 tablespoons SugarTwin® brown sugar substitute
    2 cups cooked rice

Mix thoroughly.

Pour into 4 individual baking dishes. Bake at 350° for 30 minutes or until knife comes out clean.

◆ WEDNESDAY NIGHT PUDDING ◆

1/4 cup diet cream soda
1 package unflavored gelatin
1/2 teaspoon vanilla extract
4 packets Equal® sweetener
2 cups crushed pineapple in its own juice
2 cups plain low-fat yogurt

EXCHANGES

Each serving:
　　1 fruit exchange
　　1 milk exchange

A special mid-week treat for the family.

In a saucepan:
  1/4 cup diet cream soda
  1 package unflavored gelatin
  1/2 teaspoon vanilla extract

Heat stirring until dissolved. Remove from heat and cool.

Add:
  4 packets Equal® sweetener
  2 cups crushed pineapple in its own juice

Mix until blended and refrigerate until soft set.

Add: 2 cups plain low-fat yogurt
Gently fold in.

Divide into 4 dessert dishes. Refrigerate until ready to serve.

◆ APRICOT RICE PUDDING ◆

16 halves unsweetened canned apricots
2 cups cooked rice
1 envelope sugar-free vanilla pudding
1 cup skim milk
1/2 cup evaporated skim milk
4 egg yolks
1/4 teaspoon salt
1 teaspoon vanilla
4 egg whites
3 packets Equal® sweetener

EXCHANGES

Each serving:
1 protein exchange
1 bread exchange
1 fruit exchange
1 milk exchange
1 tablespoon whipped cream = 50 extra calories

Need a dessert? Your company will rave, ooh, and aah!

Prepare:
- 16 halves, unsweetened canned apricots, chopped
- 2 cups cooked rice, prepared with 8 tablespoons juice from canned apricots as part of liquid needed

In a saucepan:
- 1 envelope sugar-free vanilla pudding
- 1 cup skim milk
- 1/2 cup evaporated skim milk
- 4 egg yolks, beaten
- 1/4 teaspoon salt
- 1 teaspoon vanilla

Cook and stir with whisk over medium heat until mixture thickens and bubbles. Remove from heat and cool.

In a small bowl:
- 4 egg whites
- 3 packets Equal® sweetener

Beat until soft peaks form. Fold egg whites into pudding mixture. Fold in apricots and rice.

Divide evenly into crystal stemware and refrigerate. Top with whipped cream (optional).

◆ GRANDMA'S CHOCOLATE ◆ RAISIN BREAD PUDDING

4 eggs, beaten
1 1/2 cups evaporated skim milk
1 package chocolate flavored low-calorie milk beverage
2 teaspoons cinnamon
Dash nutmeg
3 teaspoons reduced calorie vegetable oil margarine
1/2 teaspoon vanilla
2 tablespoons SugarTwin® brown sugar substitute
4 slices raisin bread

EXCHANGES

Each serving:
        1 protein exchange
        1 bread exchange
        1 milk exchange
        1 fat exchange

So good—a good take-along breakfast.

In a bowl:

   4 eggs, beaten
   1 1/2 cups evaporated skim milk
   1 package chocolate flavored low-calorie milk beverage

Beat with a whisk until smooth.

Add:

   2 teaspoons cinnamon
   Dash nutmeg
   3 teaspoons reduced calorie vegetable oil margarine which has
      been melted over low heat
   1/2 teaspoon vanilla
   2 tablespoons SugarTwin® brown sugar substitute
   4 slices raisin bread, torn in small pieces

Mix thoroughly. Set aside for 10 minutes to allow bread to absorb moisture. Pour into 4 individual baking dishes. Bake at 350° for 30 minutes or until knife comes out clean.

♦ A PEACH OF A STRATA ♦

2 egg yolks, beaten
2 eggs, beaten
1/3 cup SugarTwin® brown sugar substitute
1 teaspoon cinnamon
1/2 teaspoon nutmeg
2 cups skim milk
8 slices whole wheat bread
4 medium-sized fresh peaches
1 tablespoon lemon juice
1/2 cup raisins

EXCHANGES

Each serving:
    1/2 protein exchange
    1 bread exchange
    1 fruit exchange
    1/4 milk exchange

Like a pudding only deliciously better. Wonderful cold out of the refrigerator.

In a large bowl:
  2 egg yolks, beaten
  2 eggs, beaten
  1/3 cup SugarTwin® brown sugar substitute
  1 teaspoon cinnamon
  1/2 teaspoon nutmeg
  2 cups skim milk

Combine.

Add: 8 slices whole wheat bread, cubed. Let stand for 10 minutes.

In a small bowl:
  4 medium-sized fresh peaches, peeled, pitted and coarsely
    chopped
  1 tablespoon lemon juice

Toss.

Add: 1/2 cup raisins

Add to bread mixture and mix well. Pour into 1 1/2 qt. baking dish, sprayed with nonstick cooking spray. Bake at 350° for 1 hour or until knife comes out clean.

◆ APPLE BETSY ◆

4 small Granny Smith apples
3 tablespoons SugarTwin® brown sugar substitute
2 tablespoons raisins
1 teaspoon lemon juice
1/2 teaspoon cinnamon
1/3 cup plus 2 teaspoons whole wheat flour
1/2 teaspoon baking powder
2 tablespoons plus 2 teaspoons reduced calorie vegetable
    margarine
1/4 teaspoon cinnamon
1/2 cup plain low-fat yogurt
1 packet Equal® sweetener
1/8 teaspoon cinnamon

EXCHANGES

Each serving:
   1/2 bread exchange
   1 fruit exchange
   1 fat exchange
   1/4 milk exchange
   15 extra calories

A wonderful old American dish made easy for busy times. Enjoy it tonight.

In a medium-sized bowl:

    4 small Granny Smith apples, cored, pared, and cut into slices
    3 tablespoons SugarTwin® brown sugar substitute
    2 tablespoons raisins
    1 teaspoon lemon juice
    1/2 teaspoon cinnamon

Stir to combine. Divide equally into 4 individual baking dishes, sprayed with nonstick cooking spray.

In a small bowl:

    1/3 cup plus 2 teaspoons whole wheat flour
    1/2 teaspoon baking powder
    2 tablespoons plus 2 teaspoons reduced calorie vegetable
        margarine
    1/4 teaspoon cinnamon

With pastry blender or 2 knives (scissor style), cut margarine until mixture resembles coarse crumbs. Sprinkle evenly over apples in dishes. Bake at 375° for 30–35 minutes.

In a small bowl:

    1/2 cup plain low-fat yogurt
    1 packet Equal® sweetener
    1/8 teaspoon cinnamon

Mix well.

To serve, spoon 2 tablespoons yogurt mixture on warm apples.

◆ UPSIDE DOWN APRICOT ◆ COBBLER CAKE
With Vanilla Sauce

9 medium-sized fresh apricots
2 tablespoons SugarTwin® brown sugar substitute
1 tablespoon cornstarch
1/2 teaspoon grated lemon zest or peel
1/8 teaspoon nutmeg
1 cup plus 2 tablespoons whole wheat flour
1 teaspoon baking powder
1/8 teaspoon salt
1 large egg
3/4 cup buttermilk
Vanilla Sauce
1 cup plain low-fat yogurt
6 packets Equal® sweetener
4 teaspoons vanilla extract

EXCHANGES

Each serving:
    1 bread exchange
    3/4 fruit exchange
    1/2 milk exchange
    12 extra calories

A summer delight to have until the last fresh apricot fades from view!

Prepare 9 medium-sized fresh apricots by cutting into 6 wedges (leave peel on). Arrange, peel side down, in circles, starting at center in a 9-inch round baking pan, sprayed with nonstick cooking spray.

In a small bowl:

   2 tablespoons SugarTwin® brown sugar substitute
   1 tablespoon cornstarch
   1/2 teaspoon grated lemon zest or peel
   1/8 teaspoon nutmeg

Stir to combine. Sprinkle over apricots.

In a large bowl:

   1 cup plus 2 tablespoons whole wheat flour
   1 teaspoon baking powder
   1/8 teaspoon salt

Stir with whisk to combine.

In a small bowl:

   1 large egg
   3/4 cup buttermilk

Beat to combine. Add to flour mixture. Stir to moisten all ingredients. Spread over apricots with spatula.

Bake at 375° for 35–40 minutes until browned and edge has pulled away from side of pan. Cool in pan on a rack for 15 minutes. Invert onto serving plate.

VANILLA SAUCE

   1 cup plain low-fat yogurt
   6 packets Equal® sweetener
   4 teaspoons vanilla extract

Stir to combine thoroughly. Refrigerate until ready to use.
To serve, cut cake into 6 wedges and top equally with vanilla sauce.

·6·

Muffins

◆ NECTARINE TEACAKES ◆

1/2 cup softened reduced calorie vegetable oil margarine
1/3 cup SugarTwin® brown sugar substitute
1 egg
1 3/4 cups minus 1 tablespoon whole wheat flour
4 teaspoons baking powder
1 teaspoon salt
1/2 teaspoon each allspice and ginger
1 cup skim milk
3 small fresh nectarines

E X C H A N G E S

Each serving:
   3/4 bread exchange
   1/4 fruit exchange
   1 fat exchange
   14 extra calories

Fresh nectarines all summer long make these teacakes available often. Freeze ahead for greater availability.

In a large bowl:
    1/2 cup softened reduced calorie vegetable oil margarine
    1/3 cup SugarTwin® brown sugar substitute

Cream until fluffy.

Add: 1 egg, beaten

Beat in to blend.

In a medium-sized bowl:
    1 3/4 cups minus 1 tablespoon whole wheat flour
    4 teaspoons baking powder
    1 teaspoon salt
    1/2 teaspoon each allspice and ginger

Mix with whisk. Add to egg mixture gradually, alternating with:
    1 cup skim milk

Stir in: 3 small fresh nectarines, chopped

Spoon batter into 12 cup (2 1/2 inch) muffin tin, sprayed with non stick cooking spray. Bake at 400° for 20 minutes. Cool on rack for 15 minutes; then turn out onto rack to cool bottoms.

◆ FRUITY OATMEAL BRAN MUFFINS ◆

1/2 cup raisins
2 apples
1 tablespoon baking soda
1 cup water
3/4 cup whole wheat flour
3 tablespoons SugarTwin® brown sugar substitute
1 tablespoon baking powder
1/4 teaspoon salt
1 1/2 cups unprocessed bran
1/2 cup uncooked quick oats
6 tablespoons dry buttermilk powder
1 cup water
2 tablespoons vegetable oil
3 eggs

EXCHANGES

Each serving:
1/4 protein exchange
1 bread exchange
1//2 fruit exchange
1/4 milk exchange
1/2 fat exchange

Keep some in the freezer for a quick breakfast.

In a saucepan:
    1/2 cup raisins
    2 apples, cored and finely diced
    1 tablespoon baking soda
    1 cup water

Bring to boil, cover, remove from heat. Set aside 20 minutes.

In a large bowl:
    3/4 cup whole wheat flour
    2 tablespoons SugarTwin® brown sugar substitute
    1 tablespoon baking powder
    1/4 teaspoon salt

Stir with whisk to combine.

Add:
    1 1/2 cups unprocessed bran
    1/2 cup uncooked quick oats

Stir thoroughly.

In a blender jar:
    6 tablespoons dry buttermilk powder
    1 cup water
    2 tablespoons vegetable oil
    3 eggs
    1 tablespoon SugarTwin® brown sugar substitute

Blend on high speed until thoroughly mixed.

Add to flour mixture and stir to moisten. Add raisins and apples with any remaining liquid. Stir to combine.

Spray 12 cup (2 1/2 inch) muffin tin with nonstick cooking spray. Spoon equal amounts of mixture into muffin tin. Bake at 375° - 400° for 20 minutes.

◆ BLUEBERRY DELIGHT ◆

1 1/2 cups whole wheat flour
1/2 cup SugarTwin® brown sugar substitute
1 tablespoon baking powder
1/2 teaspoon salt
1 1/2 cups fresh blueberries
1 egg
1 1/2 cups plain low-fat yogurt
1/2 cup reduced calorie vegetable oil margarine

EXCHANGES

Each serving:
   3/4 bread exchange
   1/4 fruit exchange
   1 fat exchange
   1/4 milk exchange
   6 extra calories

Take advantage of summer with fresh berries or anytime with unsweetened frozen berries partially thawed. For a change make this into a coffee cake. Bake for 30–35 minutes.

In a large bowl:
    1 1/2 cups whole wheat flour
    1/2 cup SugarTwin® brown sugar substitute
    1 tablespoon baking powder
    1/2 teaspoon salt

Mix with a whisk.

Add: 1 1/2 cups fresh blueberries

Gently toss to coat.

In a small bowl:
    1 egg
Beat with fork.

Add:
    1 1/2 cups plain low-fat yogurt
    1/2 cup reduced calorie vegetable oil margarine, melted

Beat until combined. Add to flour mixture. Stir until all ingredients are moistened. Fill 12 cup (2 1/2 inch) muffin pan. Bake at 400° for 20–25 minutes or until wooden pick comes out clean.

◆ OAT BRAN MUFFINS ◆

1/4 cup raisins
1 cup boiling water
2 cups oat bran
1/3 cup nonfat dry powdered milk
1 tablespoon baking powder
1/2 cup SugarTwin® brown sugar substitute
3 eggs, beaten
1 cup plain low-fat yogurt
2 tablespoons vegetable oil
raisins and liquid

E X C H A N G E S

Each serving:

    1/4 protein exchange
    1/2 bread exchange
    1/4 milk exchange
    1/2 fruit exchange
    1/2 fat exchange

Oat bran is recommended for lowering cholesterol. Might as well make it taste good, too!

In a small bowl:
  1/4 cup raisins
  1 cup boiling water
Set aside.

In a large bowl:
  2 cups oat bran
  1/3 cup nonfat dry powdered milk
  1 tablespoon baking powder
  1/2 cup SugarTwin® brown sugar substitute
Stir with a whisk to mix.

Add:
  3 eggs, beaten
  1 cup plain low-fat yogurt
  2 tablespoons vegetable oil
Blend to combine all ingredients.

Add: raisins and liquid

Fold into egg mixture. Spoon into 12-cup (2 1/2 inch) muffin pan. Bake at 375° for 20 minutes or until lightly browned.

◆ CARROT BUTTERMILK MUFFINS ◆

1 cup minus 1 tablespoon whole wheat flour
1/2 cup unprocessed bran
1 teaspoon cinnamon
1/2 teaspoon salt
1 teaspoon baking powder
1/2 teaspoon baking soda
1/4 cup SugarTwin® brown sugar substitute
1 egg, beaten
1 1/2 cups buttermilk
2 tablespoons vegetable oil
1 teaspoon vanilla
1 1/2 cups grated carrots

E X C H A N G E S

Each serving:
    3/4 bread exchange
    1/4 milk exchange
    3/4 fat exchange
    9 extra calories

Serves 8

How can something so good be so good for you?

In a large bowl:
    1 cup minus 1 tablespoon whole wheat flour
    1/2 cup unprocessed bran
    1 teaspoon cinnamon
    1/2 teaspoon salt
    1 teaspoon baking powder
    l/2 teaspoon baking soda
    1/4 cup SugarTwin® brown sugar substitute

Stir with whisk to combine.

In a small bowl:
    1 egg, beaten

Add:
    1 1/2 cups buttermilk
    2 tablespoons vegetable oil
    1 teaspoon vanilla

Beat with whisk. Add to flour mixture. Stir to moisten all ingredients.

Add: 1 1/2 cups grated carrots, unpeeled

Stir to incorporate all ingredients. Spoon into 8 cups of 12-cup (2 1/2 inch) muffin pan, sprayed with nonstick cooking spray. Fill empty 4 cups with water (so as not to ruin them).

Bake at 350° for 35–40 minutes. Cool on a rack in pan for 5–10 minutes, then turn out on rack upside down to cool bottoms.

·7·

International Favorites

◆ BELGIAN DESSERT WAFFLES ◆

1 1/2 cups whole wheat pastry flour
2 teaspoons baking powder
1/8 teaspoon salt
2 tablespoons SugarTwin® brown sugar substitute
2 eggs yolks
1/2 cup evaporated skim milk
3/4 cup buttermilk
1 tablespoon grated lemon rind or lemon peel
2 tablespoons plus 2 teaspoons reduced calorie vegetable oil
      margarine
2 egg whites

E X C H A N G E S

Each serving:
      1/4 protein exchange
      1 bread exchange
      1/2 fat exchange
      1/4 milk exchange

CHERRY CHEESE TOPPING

1 cup part-skim ricotta cheese
6 packets Equal® sweetener
1 teaspoon almond extract
1/2 teaspoon lemon peel

E X C H A N G E S

Each serving:
      1/2 protein exchange
      1/2 fruit exchange

Belgian waffles are a wonderful special dessert that's like a meal. How about a soup and salad dinner with waffles for dessert—Wow!

In a large bowl:
   1 1/2 cups whole wheat
      pastry flour
   2 teaspoons baking powder
   1/8 teaspoon salt
   2 tablespoons SugarTwin®
      brown sugar substitute

Mix with a whisk.

In a small bowl:
   2 eggs yolks, beat slightly

Add:
   1/2 cup evaporated skim
      milk
   3/4 cup buttermilk

Stir to blend. Add to flour mixture. Mix to blend.

Add:
   1 tablespoon grated lemon
      rind or lemon peel
   2 tablespoons plus 2
      teaspoons reduced
      calorie vegetable oil
      margarine, melted

Stir to blend.

In a medium-sized bowl:
   2 egg whites, beaten until
      almost stiff

Fold into batter.

Bake in Belgian waffle maker following directions of manufacturer. Serve with fresh fruit or see below for Cherry Cheese Topping.

CHERRY CHEESE TOPPING
In a medium-sized bowl:
   1 cup part-skim ricotta cheese
   6 packets Equal® sweetener
   1 teaspoon almond extract
   1/2 teaspoon lemon peel

Beat until smooth.

Prepare 2 cups unsweetened frozen cherries with 4 packets Equal® sweetener.

To serve, for each waffle serving, spoon on 1/2 cup cherries; top with 2 tablespoons cheese mixture.

◆ MEXICAN APPLE BURRITOS ◆

Make pastry dough (see recipe for "Apple Tarts" in this book).
4 small apples
1/2 cup water
2 tablespoons lemon juice
1/4 cup SugarTwin® brown sugar substitute
1 teaspoon apple pie spice
1 teaspoon cinnamon
1 tablespoon plus 1 teaspoon cornstarch

E X C H A N G E S

Each serving:
   1 bread exchange
   1/2 fruit exchange
   5 extra calories

It's like apple pie you can eat with your fingers.

Make pastry dough (see recipe for "Apple Tarts" in this book). Divide dough into 8 pieces. Roll each piece into a 6 inch circle.

In a saucepan:
  4 small apples, peeled and sliced
  1/2 cup water
  2 tablespoons lemon juice
  1/4 cup SugarTwin® brown sugar substitute
  1 teaspoon apple pie spice
  1 teaspoon cinnamon

Bring to a boil. Simmer 3–5 minutes.

Add: 1 tablespoon plus 1 teaspoon cornstarch dissolved in 1/2 cup water

Stir until thickened. Remove from heat. Let cool 5–10 minutes.

Divide evenly on the 4 pastry circles. Roll up each circle; pinch ends and place on baking sheet. Bake at 400° for 15–20 minutes or until lightly browned.

◆ AMERICAN SHORTCAKE ◆

9 ripe peaches
6 packets Equal®
4 cups plain low-fat yogurt
8 packets Equal®
2 teaspoons almond extract
1 3/4 cups minus 1 tablespoon whole wheat flour
4 tablespoons cornstarch
2 tablespoons SugarTwin® brown sugar substitute
4 teaspoons baking powder
1/2 teaspoon lemon zest or peel
1/4 teaspoon salt
6 tablespoons reduced calorie vegetable oil margarine
3/4 cup buttermilk

EXCHANGES

Each serving:

1 bread exchange
1 fruit exchange
1 milk exchange
1 fat exchange

For individual serving:

1 cake square cut in half (see recipe)
1 peach
1 packet Equal® sweetener (see recipe)
7 tablespoons plain low-fat yogurt
1 packet Equal® sweetener
1/2 teaspoon almond extract (see recipe)

Ummm—too good to be true. Is it summer yet?

Prepare:
    9 ripe peaches, peeled & sliced
    6 packets Equal®

Mix well and refrigerate.

Prepare:
    4 cups plain low-fat yogurt
    8 packets Equal®
    2 teaspoons almond extract

Mix well and refrigerate.

In a medium sized bowl:
    1 3/4 cups minus 1 tablespoon
        whole wheat flour
    4 tablespoons cornstarch
    2 tablespoons SugarTwin®
        brown sugar substitute

    4 teaspoons baking powder
    1/2 teaspoon lemon zest or
        peel
    1/4 teaspoon salt

Mix with a whisk to combine.

Add: 6 tablespoons reduced
calorie vegetable oil margarine

With a pastry blender or 2
knives (scissor style) cut
margarine into flour mixture
until mixture resembles coarse
crumbs.

Add: 3/4 cup buttermilk

Stir to blend.

Place dough into 8 x 8-inch inch baking dish sprayed with nonstick
cooking spray. Spread evenly with fingers.

Bake at 450° until lightly browned, about 15 minutes. Cool in dish on
rack 15 minutes. Remove from dish and finish cooling on rack.

To serve cut cake into 9 squares. Cut each square horizontally in half.
Place bottom half cut side up on plate. Place 1/2 of peaches equally on
top of cake bottom. Top equally with 1/2 yogurt mixture. Place top
half of cake on peaches and repeat procedure with remaining 1/2
peaches and 1/2 yogurt mixture.

For individual serving:
    1 cake square cut in half (see
        recipe)
    1 peach
    1 packet Equal® sweetener
        (see recipe)

    7 tablespoons plain low-fat
        yogurt
    1 packet Equal® sweetener
    1/2 teaspoon almond extract
        (see recipe)

Assemble (see recipe).

◆ ENGLISH SCONES ◆

1 cup raisins
3 cups whole wheat pastry flour
1/4 cup SugarTwin® brown sugar substitute
1 tablespoon baking powder
1 teaspoon baking soda
1/2 teaspoon salt
1/3 cup softened reduced calorie vegetable oil margarine
1 cup plain low-fat yogurt
1 egg yolk
1 egg white
water

E X C H A N G E S

Each serving:
  1 bread exchange
  1/2 fruit exchange
  1/2 fat exchange

*What a treat for an afternoon break or plan them for breakfast.
Freeze remaining scones for another time.*

In a small bowl:
   1 cup raisins

Cover with boiling water; let stand 5 minutes, drain well and set aside.

In a large bowl:
   3 cups whole wheat pastry flour
   1/4 cup SugarTwin® brown sugar substitute
   1 tablespoon baking powder
   1 teaspoon baking soda
   1/2 teaspoon salt

Stir with whisk to combine.

Add: 1/3 cup softened reduced calorie vegetable oil margarine
Cut into flour mixture until mixture resembles coarse crumbs.

Add: raisins

In a small bowl:
   1 cup plain low-fat yogurt
   1 egg yolk

Stir to blend. Add to flour mixture. Stir to combine all ingredients. Refrigerate for 30 minutes. Remove from refrigerator and turn out onto a lightly floured surface. With moist hands, knead gently 10 to 12 strokes. Again with moist hands, shape 16 rounds on baking sheet, sprayed with non-stick cooking spray.

In a small bowl:
   1 egg white

Beat slightly and brush tops of scones. Bake at 425° for 15–18 minutes until lightly browned. Cool on rack.

·8·

Extra Special Extra

✦ APRICOT NOODLE KUGEL ✦

1 cup plain low-fat yogurt
1 cup part-skim milk ricotta cheese
1/3 cup SugarTwin®, brown sugar substitute
1/4 cup reduced calorie vegetable oil margarine
2 eggs
32 large dried apricot halves
4 cups fine egg noodles

--- **E X C H A N G E S** ---

Each serving:
   1 bread exchange
   l fruit exchange
   1/4 milk exchange
   3/4 fat exchange

An "old world" Jewish-style dish, wonderfully delicious for modern times. Equally good for breakfast as it is for a dessert. Make your mouth happy today. So easy to make!

Combine:
   1 cup plain low-fat yogurt
   1 cup part-skim milk ricotta cheese
   1/3 cup SugarTwin® brown sugar substitute
   1/4 cup reduced calorie vegetable oil margarine,
      melted and cooled
   2 eggs

Beat until smooth.

Add: 32 large dried apricot halves, coarsely chopped
4 cups fine egg noodles, cooked and drained

Fold in until completely combined.

Pour into 2-quart baking dish which has been sprayed with a nonstick cooking spray.

Bake at 350° for 45 minutes or until lightly browned and firm in the center.

Serve warm or cold.

NEED MORE COPIES ?

For Relatives
For Colleagues
For Patients
For Friends

Send Check or Money Order to:
Quickline Publications
P. O. Box 23362
Pleasant Hill, CA 94523-0362

For Mail Orders, Including Postage and Handling, Send:
$7.50 (single copy)
$7.00 (each, 5 to 10 copies)

For Larger Quantities, Write for Pricing

Your
Name:_____

Address_____

City_____State_____Zip_____

Number of copies to be sent to above address_____

Send Gift Order(s) to:

Name_____

Address_____

City_____State_____Zip_____

Sign Gift Card "From _____"

Name_____

Address_____

City_____State_____Zip_____

Sign Gift Card "From _____"